THE HEART OF IT

ACKNOWLEDGEMENTS

Versions of the following poems have been published previously:
'L'inconnue de la Seine', 'Montefegatesi', 'Roquebrun' in *TEN*,
Bloodaxe Books 2010; 'False Bay, Cape Town' in *Poetry Review*,
Volume 101:3 Autumn 2011; 'The Half-Mad Aunt' in *Collective
Brightness*, Sibling Rivalry Press 2011; 'Operation Cast Lead' in *The
Arvon International Poetry Competition Anthology 2010*, Aldgate Press
2010.

I am grateful to Spread the Word for including me in the Complete
Works Development Programme 2008-2010 and to the Arts Council for awarding me a grant in October 2010 to complete this
collection.

Special thanks are due to Mimi Khalvati who has been my mentor on
the journey to the completion of this collection and who has given me
encouragement, inspiration, rigorous feedback and her love and
support.

For Kate
and my grandgirls
Annie & Lily

SENI SENEVIRATNE

THE HEART OF IT

PEEPAL TREE

First published in Great Britain in 2012
Peepal Tree Press Ltd
17 King's Avenue
Leeds LS6 1QS
UK

ISBN 13: 9781845231903

Supported by
ARTS COUNCIL
ENGLAND

CONTENTS

I

II

I

EACH NIGHT

After the last remnants of the day dissolve
she turns off every light and feels her way

beyond the kitchen door into the dark.
No matter what the time of year, no matter

whether the moon is out, she picks her way
down three stone steps.

"Where have you been all night?"
the grass grumbles as she lies down.

Its dew chills through her clothes.
She spreads her arms, stares at the sky.

She has read somewhere
stars are always in pairs, locked

in a gravitational embrace.
She likes the sound of that.

RESEARCHING MY HEART

Scientists tell me my heart's four chambers
are merely muscular pouches and hold no secrets.

Four valves – tricuspid, mitral, aortic, pulmonary
– execute its double circuit circulation.

Though it has nerves, the question of feelings,
they imply, is irrelevant no matter how many

saxophones are playing. I think my heart's
too fanciful, too highly-strung to be of use

to science. See how it exaggerates its auricles,
pretends to be a hieroglyph, wraps itself in silk

and silver icicles, injects old wounds with mercury
from cinnabar, pampers its losses in gold leaf,

reaches out, membranes like groping fingers
criss-crossed with filigrees of lymph lace.

Tear open my chest. See, I have a heart like
Hanuman. There are two lovers crouching inside.

FALSE BAY, CAPE TOWN

And how do I rinse out the Indian ocean blue of her?
Is it as obvious as following the cycles of the moon

or burning sandalwood and chamomile to wake up
one day and not think of her, to redraw the line of trees

on Signal Hill? I sleep with an arched back and bent knees,
my feet in starting blocks all night. And what I have to say

is spilled paint on the highway, the footprints of a bird
without wings, the crickle of bamboo against a window pane,

a kiss in a doorway in an etching of Venice. I'm heading for
the Bridge of Sighs and the space anyone might fall back into.

The present persists, so light of things and yet so heavy.
I wear my disappointments like a coat. It has many pockets.

I am a woman who loves small berries, rough seas keep me
away from harbour walls. The wind is up. The boats are not in.

I tell the astrologer my plans are broken water barrels, she tells me
to sing in Sanskrit and wait for the wind's pull. I ride the coastal train.

There's a boy with bright eyes, a blind man playing a keyboard
in the aisles for money. You can tell so much from an iris

or the veins in an open leaf. And days like this, I make bowls –
there's a place for everything, even a dancing woman with no arms.

I am a drooping cormorant on a lime-green vase and the only way
I know the hadeda from the sacred ibis is by the sound of its crying.

HEART PROBLEMS

Ghost Frogs, more often heard
than seen, live in a landscape
where rocks huddle like petrified
figures in the fynbos.

Their mating call must in some
subconscious way remind me
of the beep, beep, beep of an
electrocardiogram because

as I climb, I hold my palm
against my chest in the V-neck
of my vest and my doctor friend
becomes alarmed. She asks me

if I'm having problems with my heart.
"If only a defibrillator could fix this
unmooring," I say, "I'd dance forever
in the mountain with the singing frogs."

ROQUEBRUN

On such an early morning in July,
a woman would have walked
the river path, past the silent frogs
still drowsy in the undergrowth,
would have seen the village houses
up ahead clinging to the cliffs,
then walked faster than the river's flow
towards the smell of baking bread.

What's altered isn't just the dream
that disappeared in the shaft of sunlight
spilling through the shutters where
I watched the flies spin a dizzy dance,
but the way I noticed that I noticed
for the first time hanging figs, spiked coats
on unripe chestnuts and bleeding hearts
crowding the river's edge.

MONTEFEGATESI

Late September and still hot. The door's creak
echoes as we step into the cool of candle wax
and faded incense. Who built such tiny churches
high in cobbled villages, statues filling every corner?

Death has been up close all year. On the journey
a winding road dropped perilously to one side
and we held our breath, not so much praying
as remembering the beliefs of those we'd lost.

Now, as the sun shines through the colours
of Judgement Day above the marble altar,
Our Lady of Perpetual Succour holds out her arms.
We walk towards her, light candles for our dead.

THE POET'S ROOM

Let's say she doesn't have a room as such
but travels from room to room across the world,
determined as a swallow, and searches for views
through windows clouded with the heat of her breath.
The wave's crest skitters sea gulls towards the rocks,
a fishing boat draws near then changes course
as a rainbow slung low dissolves in the ocean.

Let's say she doesn't have a table as such
but sits beside rocks the colour of cinnamon
where parched seaweed hangs like crumpled paper.
A cormorant dives for fish in blue that recalls
lagoons where she once swam – another life.
A boy whistles for seals and names them – Bella,
Rosa, Tina. She doesn't know how many names
there are for blue nor which one fits this sea.

And she doesn't have a lamp but distant beaches
glow like strip lights and the fluke of a whale flashes
out of the surf. Like the whale in a West Coast bay
in one September spring – how its low song stitched
their slow days. Now she stays close to harbour walls
where rocks, cut like arrows, point in all directions.

Let's say she has time but can't write in a room
if the next room is empty. A moon comes out,
she calls it drowsy, nestles between night thoughts
and morning pages. She's retreating from days
when double negatives – *It's not that I don't* – were
rusted bolts closing windows against the storm.

IN WHICH I REPAIR TO ROME

Next time Venus calls, I'll put her on hold,
in the meantime I've come to Rome with
Ovid and his Metamorphoses. In the space
between trains even destinations can change.

In the Villa Borghese, under a cedar of Lebanon,
I hear a woman tell her husband she can't cope.
She digs into her canvas bag for eye drops,
squeezes them — tears going in the wrong direction.

A poodle passes and seems to lift her spirits,
the way dogs do for some people. She sighs.
There are boats sailing at the hem of her skirt
on a rose-pink river. In her heyday she probably

learned the Louvre from end to end, now it's all
she can do to flick through her *Rough Guide to Rome*.
Sometimes I think I'll never be well again, she says
and worries her fingers against the metal fretwork.

There can be no stories of unchanging bliss.
Love is an ice cream and if on some coastlines
the sea collides and swells with a river,
it doesn't mean they will grow old together.

AUTUMN IN NEW YORK

The waitress in a diner
on 5th Avenue knows all
there is to know about
fast love. She's had enough

of tourists gawping at
the skyscrapers who only
want to eat pastrami on rye
because they're in Manhattan

and feel like it's a movie –
all the yellow taxi cabs
and NYPD hanging on
street corners. She's leaning

on the bar polishing a tired
dream of buying oysters
in a Paris market, touching
fingers with a French lover

who promises *une nuit d'amour*
and she is thinking how it will be
such slow love and like an opera,
full of endless recitatives.

THIS WOULD HAVE BEEN A LOVE POEM

It was a place whose name I forget.
The moon wasn't up, the coast a distance

over fields, ruined castle on an outcrop,
the sky like a dance and everything fading.

We were drinking German beer, I forget
the name, we said we'd come back and eat.

A generator whirred in an outhouse, she
was writing the sky in her notebook

(on the way up the lane my hands had brushed
the fuchsia hedge so the flowers fell).

I remember her voice in the evening air,
the way we decided to have another beer.

BIG APPLE COTTAGE

Midwinter and the key was cold
under the stone when we arrived.

The next morning I made porridge
and looked for the "apple's new light"

in Neruda's love sonnet 95.
It was raining, my tooth had broken

but still I ran up the Tarmac road
out of the hamlet, past the cattle grid

to the wooden gate where I shouted
at the crows landing in the trees.

Later we walked the cliffs hugging
the coastline at Whitesands Bay.

The sea was a consolation and after,
in the café, I thought about choices

as if they were sandwich fillings and
how some days you take what comes

and others you know that nothing else
but parma ham and pecorino will do.

PAPER & GLASS

She left me in a house with hollow rooms.
My heart was paper, then my heart was glass.
Windows sealed, I asked the waning moon
to burn the seasons, choke the grate with ash.

My heart was paper, then my heart was glass.
I knew it would take time – perhaps forever
to burn the seasons, choke the grate with ash,
my tongue dust-dry and thirsty for my lover.

I knew it would take time – perhaps forever,
still trying to repair the broken things.
My tongue dust-dry and thirsty for my lover,
I was looking for a place to write her skin.

Still trying to repair the broken things,
although I feared my longing was naïve,
I was looking for a place to write her skin –
her prints still clinging to the basil leaves

(although I feared my longing was naïve),
the way she squeezed a lemon in her palm,
her prints still clinging to the basil leaves,
fingers stained with saffron, sunlight on her arm.

The way she squeezed a lemon in her palm –
why was it only remnants that survived,
fingers stained with saffron, sunlight on her arm?
Although I'd tried to coax her back to love,

why was it only remnants that survived?
windows sealed, I asked the waning moon.
Although I'd tried to coax her back to love,
she left me in a house with hollow rooms.

REASONS TO STOP LOOKING
FOR THE RIGHT WORDS

I watch the night's fingers
smudge darkness on grey gardens
rub out houses, leave
remnants of chimneys.

There is no hard and fast
boundary between light
and lightning, between almost
and it doesn't really matter.

KIND OF BLUE

There is too much still to be unsaid.
When I can't sleep, I plot my body

in colour, put blue ice agate
under my pillow to heal my throat.

There are fireballs under my ribs.
I dream of bold yellow flames

that look like Van Gogh's cornfield
threatening to burn down everything.

Someone's playing 'So What'
from the album *Kind of Blue*.

Above the music, the crackle and spit
consumes houses and willow fences.

I hurry away from this charred place,
sit under the glass-bead blossoms

of a wire baobab tree and float
pink hibiscus in a bowl of royal blue.

LOVE ME DO

It's 1968 and I'm walking with her, my best friend,
through the smoggy early dusk, arms linked,
heads together, whispering and tingling with unrequited
teenage passion, following a boy three years older,
the object of our joint desire who's just about to leave
the Catholic Grammar school for University, so there
isn't much time though we haven't worked out what
we want the time to do when we miss the Number 33
that he jumps on even though we run, weighed down
with our satchels, heavy with tonight's homework
which we'll finish later after we've shared our panting
disappointments on the top deck of the next bus home
and stretched out head to head on her bedroom floor
listening to John Lennon who we are also in love with,
singing *Ask Me Why,* the B side of *Love me Do*.

RED ROOM

My heart is a red room, piled high
with bric-a-brac. The clock on the wall

has stopped long ago and a plaster owl
is trying not to look at the raffle drum

still spinning. From somewhere
underneath the clutter I can hear the crackle

of Billie Holiday on vinyl; and on the floor,
next to my worn-out running shoes,

scraps of paper that could be love notes
are hiding inside fifteen fragile paper cones.

STARDUST

It could be any city
with stars falling

on the parking lot,
a man too busy polishing

his Cadillac to notice
and a baby at the window

of a high rise building
laughing at the light.

THE FAMOUS BLUE RAINCOAT

Oh, but it is noisy this City Library today, in a way that libraries
never used to be, what with the beep outside of a lorry in reverse,

the squeak of book trolleys on the move and even the librarians, who
always used to be the ones saying *Quiet Please,* talking in corners

while I count the squares on a frosted glass ceiling, savour the taste
of Green & Blacks chocolate (70% dark) as I listen to a song

of Leonard Cohen's playing in my head, the one about his brother
who's on drugs until I reach the line about the famous blue raincoat,

which starts me thinking about those blue jeans of yours and how
I watched you pull them on this morning, the wardrobe doors flung

wide open, you staring inside as if you had lost something, before you
pulled that red t-shirt (the one I bought you last summer) over your head,

me in bed, wanting to kiss your neck, barely visible between the t-shirt
and your hairline, and how, since you had just come from the shower,

I noticed everything about you had a newly-washed smell but I couldn't
recognise the fragrance though it lingered even after you rushed out,

without looking, with that brown leather bag on your shoulder (the one
you found in the second-hand shop) and how your goodbye left me

longing for the way you used to catch your thumb on the edge of those
goodbye smiles you used to direct at me and how all that may change

because last night you told me you've got plans to be on your own now,
which is why I'm sitting in the City Library today, thankful for the noise

and Leonard Cohen and his brother, the one with the blue raincoat who maybe one day came back to see him, after such a beautiful song, signed

sincerely, L. Cohen.

NO ADJECTIVES

When you wake up and feel yourself in that place between
sleep and consciousness, thinking you have to get a new bed

because this one is restless with the wrong dreams, then you are
doing that thing of looking for practical solutions to something

called heartache because last night you fell asleep on a question,
same question, because something trapped in your chest trying

to get out, call it a sob for now, is more insistent than the sun
through the gap in the blinds and asks to be noticed, asks you

to say "poor thing" before you get up and there are no adjectives
or practical solutions to change this bed, this room, this longing.

DECEMBER

We hung red baubles
on my squat, pot-grown

Christmas tree last night
and this morning my granddaughter

talked about the way dreams
are in pieces and you don't know

which bits come where.
I need a fire now to brighten

the marble mantelpiece.
The medicine bottle is full

beside the half empty
wine bottle and the flowers

in the tumbler are the last
surviving daisies.

SHE HAD HONEYBEES

She had honeybees with golden eyes
who left lotus leaves at her door to woo her.
They stained her lips with nectar,
cocooned her in silk and wax.

When the bee-eaters came hunting,
the honeybees fled, scattering pollen
on the trunks of hollow trees to mark
the way back home, but never returned.

She followed their trail, found them hiding
in the mouth of a cave. Her tongue,
viscous with the loss of them, called out,

"Come home, my honeybees."
But their terror was blind to her love,
their stings merciless in the swarm.

THE RELIABLE ELEGANCE OF NUMBERS

I think I have a perfect angle on
the relation between two idealised bees

with honey in mind, who skim
the surface with heads full of hexagons,

collect pine cones, count the florets
in sunflowers. But the closed form,

without solution, leads to the divisibility
sequence. No more golden ratios.

The negative index sets in with irrational
constructions and though linear recursion

implies it is possible to turn back, I find
I'm going the wrong way round in spirals,

trying to believe that the art of subtraction
can create another life beyond zero.

EASTER SUNDAY

It is a good day to consider transformation,
as if it were a resurrection from the dead,

a rolling away of stone, a walk on dry grass
with no voice under an aching blue sky,

to stand on a broken gate and watch a hawk
take the last drink of death and never rise again.

A pelargonium's unseasonal flowering
smells of benediction and belief as I hover

over last year's pursuit of weeping. And look,
after years of sodden summers that threatened

its existence, the Adonis Blue butterfly, making
a cautious comeback, is poised above the vetch.

II

L'INCONNUE DE LA SEINE

There was a swell on the surface of the Seine that day
making faces at me. So I blew kisses at an open mouth

and whispered, "Drown me peaceful, drown me slow."
I wanted the time, you see, to float undead through Paris.

I could have choked on a glass of milk as a child
and missed this opportunity. Don't call it suicide

as if it's a tragedy. This was the first time in my life
I had been in control of anything. Imagine, not dying

but dissolving, becoming a river. Was I afraid?
Not of the fall. I was afraid of the Water Police,

the way they walk along the river, any one of them
could have seen me floating, but nightfall saved me.

Before the river had me, I had one last look at the stars
"Just look at you," I said, "already dead and still shining."

PIANO MAN

April 7th 2005, he stepped wordless
out of the sea at Sheerness,
no labels on his formal suit and tie,

arms dripping limp against his sides,
everything about him loose, dishevelled,
except his eyes unflinching wide.

They found him wandering that day
like a traveller without a way
to lose, without a map or compass.

To him their questions in the milky light
were like bubbles rising underwater
as if his near-drowning was not over

and the sea still held his swaying body
as he cursed the swell of salty water
when it buoyed him up for he was ready

then to lose himself and thought the ache
that lay like boulders in his chest would
pull him underneath the ocean's weight.

But tidal currents dumped him on dry ground
where strangers probed for answers but his voice
jammed deep inside his larynx made no sound.

What else to do with one whose silence might imply
mute desperation or defiance but take him to a hospital
to be observed, then let the papers modify

his story so it pandered to the public's need
to settle this unsettling man in a familiar frame
of place of birth, belonging, history and name?

The things we know for sure: They give him
pen and paper. They hope he'll write the facts.
He draws a grand piano and a Swedish flag.

The piano's etched in ballpoint pen;
its lid like a tsunami towers
above the lines he's scratched as markers

for the strings in equal number to the keys
and in the spotlight is a vacant stool above a shadow
lurking where the pianist's feet would be.

His social worker says it is amazing how
they take him to the chapel and he sits down
at the holy ivories and plays for several hours

a repertoire that spans a range from Lennon to Tchaikovsky.
But he can only feel his fingertips brush velvet,
hover in the air then drop like diamond onto vinyl,

lifting sound that curls and dives, then bends
beneath curved arches, melting into pools
where knotted strings of light tie up loose ends

and loop them back in concertina'd swirls
of stammered notes until his fingers
are no longer fingers but a band of cells

playing out the rhythms of his splintered self.
The media play a different tune and dub him
the Piano Man, the virtuoso mute musician

who has jammed the National Missing Persons
Helpline as they field the calls. Rome calls Interpol
with word from Darius, a street artist from Poland,

that this is sure to be a French musician he has met
in Nice. Friends of missing Geoff from Dallas bet
that if someone checks his website there is sure

to be a likeness and the fact that Geoff's an actor
can explain his excellent performance in the role,
but that and all the other leads go cold.

Experts armed with favourite diagnoses wonder
if he is autistic, schizophrenic or clinically depressed,
while doctors speculate that his voice box is removed

and examine possibilities of vocal chord paralysis
provoked by cancer, stroke or whiplash injury
precipitated by a fall out of a boat into the sea

and while they search for more appropriate medicine
than music, Piano Man throws notes like pebbles in a well
and listens to the story in the echoes of their fall.

Most nights he curls himself into the shape of dreams
along the water's edge and coils his body like an eel
in hollowed places in the sand to watch his drowning,

then mornings stares at bowls of sugared cereal,
licks his lips with salted tongue and cannot hear
sounds above his water line as a nurse appeals,
Is this the day you're going to speak to me?

SAFETY PLAN

I hide in the walls when
the shouting starts. I blow
three times. A tunnel opens.

It smells of picnics and cut
grass, soft like a winter woolly.
There's only me knows

the code to get there,
*Oranges and lemons, oranges
and lemons, let me pass.*

This time when she finds me,
she stares with big eyes
all puffy and red. Her voice

is kind of cheerful like pale
sunshine and she asks
me what I want for tea.

But there's a monster
trampeding in my head all
mixed up with broken glass,

dead poppies and water
drip, dripping on the floor
and if my voice wasn't still

lost in the tunnel somewhere
I'd say, *Oranges –
oranges and lemons.*

OBESE HEDGEHOG PUT ON STARVATION DIET

They label our cages with made-up names.
There's Spud, the spikeless lad next door
who's always known at heart he was a guinea pig,
but men in rubber gloves have other plans.

He's been inside two years – skin grafts,
biopsies, you name it. They've got him on
daily rubdown now, special oils to grow
new spines. He rejects them every time.

I'm known as George the Football, hey
don't laugh, I know I'm overweight but
life's hard at the arse-end of the food chain,
can't find a fresh beetle for love nor money.

There's badgers if we venture far afield,
and roads where cars conspire to turn us
into jokes so we rummage through junk food
in gardens where the slugs are full of poison.

If you think lawn mowers are our biggest risk,
then think again. Our greatest fear is hibernation –
nest destruction, cold and floods. It took my sister's
skin and bones, drove my mother mad.

Resolved to boost my body fat, she confined me
to the nest, out of love and scared of losing me,
I guess. She foraged day and night for food;
stale peanuts, burgers, chocolate bars, old bread.

"Mam, we *are* nocturnal insect-eaters, none of this
feels right," I'd start to say, before she forced
another mouthful. Soon my teeth no longer craved
the crunch of beetle, nor my tongue the slurp of slug.

Rescued by a Wildlife volunteer, I ended up in here
like some kind of sideshow in a freak circus,
men in white coats checking my armpits for excess fat,
talking about Atkins diets, heart attacks, liver disease.

They reckon I'll be inside for six months, calling it
a slow weight-loss programme – treadmill workouts,
supervised swim sessions, and one lousy tablespoon
of cat food a day. I'd kill for a bag of crisps.

ROCKY AND ME

You know where you are with a pit-bull.
His name's Rocky. I walk him for her
next door. Lazy cow can't be bothered.
He might look fierce, giant jawbone
and a mouth that could snap a baby's
head off, but he's soft as shite.

People are pathetic. He's on a leash but
they walk past like he's about to kill.
Thing about fear is, it smells – all that sweat,
prickling your skin. It's a dead giveaway.
I flick my wrist like I'm about to let go.
You should see how they jump. Pathetic.

Bitch, my dad says, *you need slapping down,*
like your mam. As if I care. Rather be a dog
any day. I'd bite his ugly head off, stop him
gobbing off. When he starts I stare him down.
He hates that. My mam never looks him in the eye.
I'd leave tomorrow, if it weren't for Rocky.

Besides which, I've got scores to settle at school.
They're all written down in a book. Slashed a hole
in my mattress to hide it. First page goes:
Tracey – bang head against playground wall
Paula – give her a bloody good kicking
Kim – take a Stanley knife to her legs or face.

I haven't touched anyone yet. But I will.
I'll do it. One day. When they least expect it.
A sudden letting go of the leash.

THE HALF-MAD AUNT

Never old enough for her age, they called her
the half-mad aunt. Instead of saris, she wore
blouses with skirts hooped like crinolines.

She was in love with the saints, John Britto
and Gonzalo Garcia, who had come with the ships
from Portugal. But they let her down.

She only wanted a carriage and white horses,
not the marriage, not the strange man each night
in her bedroom showing his body parts.

When she carved a talisman to chase away demons,
her in-laws said she was possessed, sent her back
with actual bits of saints tied in scapulars round her neck.

On the bus to Colombo she was all red lipstick
and high heels asking her embarrassed nephew,
Why are these bad spirits hammering my heart?

GOGO'S CLOCK

Her clock has numbers big enough
to see in the dim glow of the oil lamp.
It is almost six pm. The child of her child
is drumming a spoon on a cooking pot.
This is not the old age she imagined,
stiff limbs reaching to her highest shelf
for medicines that masquerade as syrup
sweet as cherry bubble-gum or leave
a bitter after-taste like ten cent coins.
Days are gripped in rigorous routines
of twice daily dosage to stop
the multiplying virus in its tracks.
She holds each syringe up close
to failing eyes, peers at millimetre
markings, waits for the clock
and the jingle of a twilight TV soap
to verify the time for coaxing
chemicals inside the child.
Mealie meal and sugar beans.
Then sleep, curled like petals
round their common loss, until
the morning breaks. The clock
says five-thirty. Time enough
to rouse and stretch her tired body,
organise the morning medication,
put the mealie porridge on to boil
and step outside. A chill in the air.
Winter on its way and with it the rains.
She has kept this seedling child
of hers alive for one full year.
How to keep her warm and dry?

THE ISLAND MOUNTAIN GLACIER ERUPTS

While my husband sleeps in Istanbul,
a sky-swallower, sky-darkener, exhales
from the mountain's mouth above our farm.

My bag is ready packed. I learned in school
how Laki made the Icelanders stop dancing,
and changed the shape of everything.

I rouse my mother, gather children, wrap
their dreams in blankets. The three-year-old,
half-waking, asks me if the sky is falling in.

Sulphur on my tongue, eyes scratched with dust,
I tread footprints through a film of ash
once, twice, three times to the car.

We drive away from melting ice-flows, leave
my farm, my cows who bellow in the barn,
my cows who wait with swollen udders.

If floods don't kill them, then ash will, already
settling on their lungs, devouring spaces
meant for breath. I should be milking now.

TESTIMONY OF BABY HAYDOVA
Beirut – 14th August 2006

In days to come I may grow older,
learn to speak the names for anger, fear, forgiveness,

but these days all I know is how my mother
holds my face so tight against her that I feel

the tremors of her heartbeat pumping through my veins.
The smell of her blood will never leave me.

Take your picture now
then tell me why I have been saved.

MY FATHER'S WAR

Beyond the flicker of his photos he walks,
khaki-clad, out of stifling dreams towards me.

His hands are younger than my own and I lean
into his chest, settle underneath his arm.

Father, was it sweet, was it noble, did you
yell or stumble? My questions pour

like liquid through the gaps between
his ribs, as I feel their rapid rise and fall.

I ran, I ran, I fell forward. I picked myself up.
I ran, I ran, I fell forward. I picked myself up.

The sky was a blanket. The sky fell on me.
The sky fell on me, but I did not sleep.

Silence then before the fumble of his arm
around my waist. I am a child in a woman's body

stretching to hold him until we are folded,
trembling together, watching fires fall on the horizon.

THIS IS WHAT I HEARD

If you do something for long enough, the world will accept it.
International law progresses through violations.
(Colonel Reisner, Israeli Army)

I heard that the Colonels had killed
the beekeepers, though they had no use
for nectar and scorned the secret wisdom
of the hives, the worship of wild flowers.

I heard that the Colonels mocked
the drones – stingless, defenceless males
doomed to search for Virgin Queens,
mate them on the wing then die.

I heard that the Colonels warned of
uprisings of arum lilies threatening
the hive's security, blooming wild
on open ground as if the land was theirs.

I heard that the Colonels cautioned
worker bees who entered pollen zones
to watch for nectar traps and armed
the drones with weapons of offence.

I heard that the Colonels sent the first
drone volunteer to fix its roving eye
on a radiant family of flora bedded
in an open courtyard and fire its missile.

I heard that the targeted explosion
burnt out the eyes of Adonis palaestina,
scattered the limbs of Artedia squamata,
crushed the heart of a Carmel daisy,

chopped in half a branched stem of hyssop,
shattered a cluster of Bellis perennis,
ripped the head and seeded offspring from
Anemone coronaria, daughter of the winds.

I heard that sap oozed, petals were thrown
against walls and clung there, perfumes
curdled over stone flags soaked in pollen
as night fell on the cemetery of flowers.

IF ONLY

She takes diazepam to numb the shape
of those lip-read messages she collides

with in the attic where the coronation tin
is full of Uncle Harry's medals.

She could spit on them or make up any story
amongst the bric-a-brac. It was easy to pluck

one red leaf and squeeze it between the pages
of old books until it resembled parchment.

And no matter what she did, no-one else
did their best. He may have died a hero

but his bones are quieter than she needs.
It was never her nerves and it could have

been otherwise if only someone had netted
the butterflies and let them speak.

WOUNDS OF WAR

The average number of completed suicides per month
by US veterans returning from Iraq & Afghanistan is 690
(Virginia Quarterly *Autumn 2008*)

There is an I in this poem who is
as silent as the startled tulips, who can't
reach the imagined chime of where was it

he was heading before, before all this dust
before all the random rocks of where
was it that he went, came from

who is unavailable, waits for, keeps waiting
for an appointment to view, looking for the mirror
in the stone to see himself again

who will enter the space between the dying yucca
that smells of old books and the jasmine tree
whose buds are like pinpricks of blood

who will hear for the last time
the sound of his own footsteps.

OPERATION CAST LEAD

She was baking bread
when the soldiers came.
Her children ran to her.

She held the two of them,
one against each hip, the dough
on her fingers stuck to their hair.

Two days and she never washed
her hands, kept thinking of the dough
still rising in the kitchen.

Now the soldiers are saying things,
jabbing at the air with guns,
fingers too near the triggers.

She thinks the guns are like
heavy limbs in the hands
of these wild-eyed boys.

If they let us go, we will
walk south, she tells herself,
walk south with everyone else.

We may not sleep tonight
nor find bread but, Insha'allah
we will stay alive.

With her hands full of children,
she moves through the space
where her door used to hang.

Her right hip rotates, lifts
her right foot, her left hip tilts
the left foot follows.

The turn, the swirl of her dress,
the squeeze of her hands
on her children's palms.

The turn, left instead of right,
the sniper's eye holding her heart
at the centre of his lens.

The moment of turning left
instead of right, the arc of a weapon
across the wide screen of this moving picture.

This woman walking, this woman
walking with her children, walking
the wrong way, too close to the red line.

This woman, her hands' grip loosened
with traces of dough on her fingers,
remnants in her children's hair.

BLOOD, BLOOD, BLOOD MAKES THE GREEN GRASS GROW

What do you expect? You take a thin-skinned boy
like mine, make fodder out of him, take everything
that's good out of him, squeeze it out like wringing
soapy water from the washing, twisting and twisting
till he's so wound-up he can't unwind himself, can't
pull himself straight, can't pull himself right again.

What could I do? He was eighteen, my thin-skinned boy.
What future did this place promise? A gaping hole of a life
blasting ore from open mines, groans like dead men's groans
from underground to disturb his dreams and hard drinking
after hard work. He either went with my blessing or without.
No son of mine is going off to war without my blessing.

Boot Camp first. They do a good job there, the army,
brainwashing, teaching them to kill, kick in people's doors,
flush them out like grouse and shoot. Drill Sergeant screams,
What makes the green grass grow? and my boy screams
Blood, blood, blood makes the green grass grow.
They took him and they hardened him. My soft son.

Whatever way I look at it, he came home from that war
with the devil at his heels, ankle-deep in bodies, all those
bodies he brought back with him, couldn't get his mind
to go to other places, kept going back to those broken roads,
nights spent looking for his own soul. But the devil had it.
I tried to wrap my arms round his despair, pull him back.

A child crushed under his tank: *He came too close, mam,*
I went over him. The lads felt the bump. Must be a dog,
I told them, mam, must be a dog. — That's not my son.
He used to go hunting as a child, always went to pick up
the rabbits. Always had respect for the dead. Not my son
to shoot an unarmed man in the forehead, in his own home.

What could I do? There's only so much a mother can do.
He'd just sit there, all the light in his eyes sputtered out.
He was all in pieces. That war cut him up, left a hole
where the devil jumped in. Came back saying he had plans
to be an alcoholic. What kind of ambition is that?
My lovely boy. He'd have been better off in the mines.

We got him a Labrador; it licked the tears from his face
at night. But in the day, he took to stoning chickens,
took to thinking Satan had more power than God.
If you don't give a shit, nothing can bother you.
I could kill every one of you and not give it a second thought.
Blood, blood, blood makes the green grass grow.

He drove down a dead-end road, took a handgun
to himself, in a forest where people strip pine boughs
for Christmas wreaths. Only twenty-three. Imagine.
Half a bottle of Jack Daniels. A penknife stabbed
through his ID. A suicide note on the back of a pistol
safety certificate, his brains blasted through the roof.

He's laid himself to rest now, found some solid ground.
And the grass grows over him, thicker every year. I want
to dig it up. Just to see him one more time. Just to get at him.
My son. All his demons still lurking under my bed each night.
"This is War", the song's called. The one he asked us to play
at his funeral. It's by a band called Smile Empty Soul.

FOR THE ELEPHANT IN THE ROOM

The elephant in the room, orphaned
by history's hunters, is hungry.

We could feed her the fruit of buffalo thorn trees
and ransack the marula tree for berries.

Her trunk could roar, purr, rumble, sneeze,
remove thorns, pick up pins, pull up bushes,

detect trip wires and traps, doodle in sand,
dowse for water and also read our faces.

Her patience is unyielding, her memory
long and the patterns on her feet leave

a mark as unique as our fingerprints but we
are not wise and we lumber on in silence.

LIFE PLANS

How do I wait in this life, on this page
with the ink of that other life leaking

through? We nearly had all the time
in the world, suddenly we had no time,

threw it away like fish guts on the quayside –
all those coloured ribbons that had plumped

up my heart unravelled out of me, blew away
in the wind. Some days I am a taxonomist

obsessed with ordering and naming the bones,
some days I write out life plans in cafés

on paper serviettes, suck at the oak leaf
on my cappuccino froth, then blow.

ABOUT THE AUTHOR

Seni Seneviratne, born and raised in Leeds, Yorkshire, is of English and Sri Lankan heritage. Her work as a poet and creative artist is widely acclaimed. She has given readings, performances, which include a capella song, and workshops in UK, Canada, South Africa, USA and Egypt.

Her debut collection, *Wild Cinnamon and Winter Skin,* was published in March 2007 by Peepal Tree Press. One of the poems from this collection was highly commended by the judges in the Forward Poetry Prize 2007. In 2008 she was selected to take part in The Complete Works a National Development Programme for Black and Asian Poets. In 2009, she was awarded a Travel Fellowship to fund an extended stay in Cape Town where she met and interviewed South African poets about the relationship between poetry and trauma and did a range of voluntary work including collaboration with a visual artist in weekly workshops to build the self esteem of residents at a shelter for abused women. In the same year, she was invited to present a paper, "Speaking the Unspeakable, The Poetry of Witness", at an international conference "Beyond Reconciliation" hosted by the University of Cape Town. In May 2010 she was selected as one of the writers on the El Gouna International Writers Residency. In September 2010 her poem "Operation Cast Lead" was shortlisted in the Arvon International Poetry Competition and she was awarded an Arts Council Grant to complete this collection, *The Heart of It.*

She has organised creative events and facilitated creative writing workshops and residences in schools, colleges and community settings working with a range of abilities and with people from a variety of experiences and backgrounds. She has been supporting survivors of trauma and abuse since the early eighties, in a voluntary capacity, as an educationalist, a trainer and since 2001 as a qualified psychotherapist in the NHS and in the voluntary sector. She currently works as a freelance writer, mentor, trainer and creative consultant. She has used her skills as a visual artist to deliver mixed media workshops.

ALSO BY SENI SENEVIRATNE

Wild Cinnamon and Winter Skin
ISBN: 9781845230500; pp. 64; pub. March 2007; price: £7.99

Seni Seneviratne's debut collection offers a poetic landscape that echoes themes of migration, family, love and loss and reflects her personal journey as a woman of Sri Lankan and English heritage.

The poems cross oceans and centuries. In "Cinnamon Roots" Seni Seneviratne travels from colonial Britain to Ceylon in the 15th century and back to Yorkshire in the 20th Century; in "A Wider View" time collapses and carries her from a 21st century Leeds back to the flax mills of the 19th century; poems like "Grandad's Insulin", based on childhood memories, place her in 1950's Yorkshire but echo links with her Sri Lankan heritage.

"Loss, love, memory, from Yorkshire to Sri Lanka and back, Seni Seneviratne's poems delve in and out of a complex history. These tender, moving poems weave a delicate web." — Jackie Kay

"There are historians that may record our experiences. And these experiences may be found in the galleries of the future. Preserved. But it's in the poetry where the exhibits actually live. And it's here. Let Seni walk you through the labarynthine gallery of Wild cinnamon and winter skin." — Lemn Sissay.

"Seni Seneviratne's poetry straddles continents and centuries – and does so with an easy fluency. The reader is drawn into her journey of discovery for her 'cinnamon roots' and her exploration of issues of identity and relationships. Personal and universal histories interweave in these poems." — Debjani Chatterjee

All Peepal Tree titles are available from the website
www.peepaltreepress.com
with a money back guarantee, secure credit card ordering
and fast delivery throughout the world at cost or less.